THE AMERICAN NEGRO
HIS HISTORY AND LITERATURE

HISTORY
OF THE NEGRO RACE
IN AMERICA
1619-1880

George W. Williams

ARNO PRESS and THE NEW YORK TIMES

NEW YORK 1968

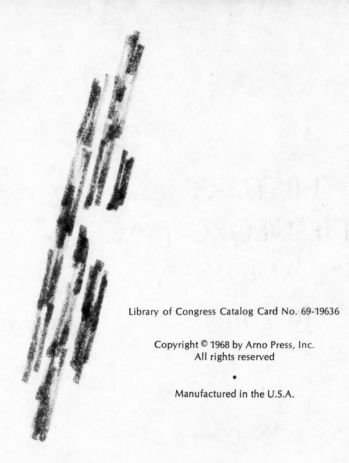

Library of Congress Catalog Card No. 69-19636

Copyright © 1968 by Arno Press, Inc.
All rights reserved

*

Manufactured in the U.S.A.

General Editor
WILLIAM LOREN KATZ

GEORGE WASHINGTON WILLIAMS, BORN OCTOBER 16, 1849 IN Bedford Springs, Pennsylvania, served in the Union Army by falsifying his age. Mustered out in 1865, he reenlisted for a short period and then joined the Mexican Army, where he became a Lieutenant-Colonel. He graduated from Howard University in 1868 and studied at Newton Theological Seminary in Massachusetts, graduating in 1874. A Baptist minister and government clerk in New England, he also started a journal, *The Commoner*, and a weekly newspaper, *The Southwestern Review*. He moved to Cincinnati, where he was again a minister, and also studied law. Williams then entered politics and in 1879 became the first Negro elected to the Ohio legislature. He wrote articles under a pen name for a white newspaper, the *Cincinnati Commercial*, and was Judge Advocate of the Grand Army of the Republic.

At the end of his term, President Arthur appointed Williams U. S. Minister to Haiti, but the incoming president, Grover Cleveland, removed him. Williams wrote a long letter to President Cleveland, asking him to be fair in resolving the case, but he failed to get the Haitian appointment.

While doing research for an oration on the contributions the Negro had made to the United States, which was to be delivered on July 4, 1876, Williams found such an abundance of materials on the Negro's achievements that he decided to record them. He retired from public life and devoted seven years to research and the writing of his two-volume *History of the Negro Race in America from 1619 to 1880*. It was published in 1883, with the subtitle *Negroes as Slaves, as Soldiers and as Citizens*.

The first volume begins with life in Africa, continues with a study of slavery in the American colonies, the Negro in the American Revolution, and slavery as a political and legal problem in the Revolution and after. The second volume covers the Negro in the War of 1812, the antislavery struggle, the results of emancipation, and the Negro exodus from the South. Although not a trained historian, Williams's studies in law and theology had taught him to research carefully and document thoroughly. His was the first history by a Negro to be given serious attention by white American scholars. It was generally praised highly and some reviewers even called Williams the Negro Bancroft.

The author then turned his attention to the Civil War, and after working for five years he produced *A History of the Negro Troops in the War of the Rebellion, 1861–65.* This heavily-documented book, also praised by critics, was probably the best work on the subject until books by Benjamin Quarles, Dudley T. Cornish and James M. McPherson were published a half century later.

Williams's emotional writing style made his work readable and interesting to his 19th Century readers, though a bit oratorical and florid for the present day. But his historical scholarship, documentation and organization of facts stand up very well indeed. *History of the Negro Race in America from 1619 to 1880* is a fine early general history of the United States Negro.

Ernest Kaiser
SCHOMBURG COLLECTION
NEW YORK PUBLIC LIBRARY

HISTORY

OF THE

NEGRO RACE IN AMERICA

Fraternally Yours,

Geo. W. Williams.

HISTORY

OF THE

NEGRO RACE IN AMERICA

FROM 1619 TO 1880.

NEGROES AS SLAVES, AS SOLDIERS, AND AS CITIZENS;

TOGETHER WITH

A PRELIMINARY CONSIDERATION OF THE UNITY OF THE HUMAN
FAMILY, AN HISTORICAL SKETCH OF AFRICA, AND AN
ACCOUNT OF THE NEGRO GOVERNMENTS OF
SIERRA LEONE AND LIBERIA.

BY

GEORGE W. WILLIAMS,

FIRST COLORED MEMBER OF THE OHIO LEGISLATURE, AND LATE JUDGE ADVOCATE OF THE
GRAND ARMY OF THE REPUBLIC OF OHIO, ETC.

IN TWO VOLUMES.

VOLUME I.

1619 TO 1800.

NEW YORK:

G. P. PUTNAM'S SONS,

27 AND 29 WEST 23D STREET.

1883.

TO THE

REV. JUSTIN DEWEY FULTON, D. D.,

OF BROOKLYN, NEW YORK;

AND TO THE

HON. CHARLES FOSTER,

GOVERNOR OF OHIO:

WHO, AS CLERGYMAN AND STATESMAN, REPRESENT THE PUREST PRINCIPLES
OF THE AMERICAN CHURCH AND STATE.

To the Illustrious Representative of the Church of Christ:

WHO, FOR A QUARTER OF A CENTURY, HAS STOOD THE INTREPID CHAMPION OF DIVINE TRUTH,
AND THE DEFENDER OF HUMANITY: DURING THE DARK DAYS OF SLAVERY, PLEADING
THE CAUSE OF THE BONDMEN OF THE LAND; DURING THE WAR, URGING
THE EQUALITY OF NEGROES AS SOLDIERS; DURING RECONSTRUCTION,
ENCOURAGING THE FREEDMEN TO NOBLE LIVES THROUGH THE
AGENCY OF THE CHURCH AND THE SCHOOL; AND EVER-
MORE THE ENEMY OF ANY DISTINCTION BASED
UPON RACE, COLOR, OR PREVIOUS CON-
DITION OF SERVITUDE.

To the Distinguished Statesman:

WHO, ENDUED WITH THE GENIUS OF COMMON SENSE, TOO EXALTED TO BE INFLAMED BY
TEMPORARY PARTY OR FACTIONAL STRIFE, AND WHO, AS CONGRESSMAN AND GOVERNOR,
IN STATE AND NATIONAL POLITICS, HAS PROVEN HIMSELF CAPABLE OF

SACRIFICING PERSONAL INTEREST TO PUBLIC WELFARE;

WHO, IN DEALING WITH THE NEGRO PROBLEM, HAS ASSERTED A NEW DOCTRINE IN
IGNORING THE CLAIMS OF RACES; AND WHO, AS THE FIRST NORTHERN GOV-
ERNOR TO APPOINT A COLORED MAN TO A POSITION OF PUBLIC TRUST,
HAS THEREBY DECLARED THAT NEITHER NATIONALITY NOR
COMPLEXION SHOULD ENHANCE OR IMPAIR THE CLAIMS
OF MEN TO POSITIONS WITHIN THE GIFT OF
THE EXECUTIVE.

TO THESE NOBLE MEN THIS WORK IS DEDICATED,

WITH SENTIMENTS OF HIGH ESTEEM AND PERSONAL REGARD, BY THEIR
FRIEND AND HUMBLE SERVANT,

THE AUTHOR.

PREFACE.

————◆————

I WAS requested to deliver an oration on the Fourth of July, 1876, at Avondale, O. It being the one-hundredth birthday of the American Republic, I determined to prepare an oration on the *American Negro*. I at once began an investigation of the records of the nation to secure material for the oration. I was surprised and delighted to find that the historical memorials of the Negro were so abundant, and so creditable to him. I pronounced my oration on the Fourth of July, 1876; and the warm and generous manner in which it was received, both by those who listened to it and by others who subsequently read it in pamphlet form, encouraged me to devote what leisure time I might have to a further study of the subject.

I found that the library of the Historical and Philosophical Society of Ohio, and the great *Americana* of Mr. Robert Clarke containing about eight thousand titles, both in Cincinnati, offered peculiar advantages to a student of American history. For two years I spent what time I could spare from professional cares in studying the whole problem of the African slave-trade; the founding of the British colonies in North America; the slave problem in the colonies; the rupture between the colonies and the British Government; the war of the Revolution; the political structure of the Continental government and Confederation; the slavery question in local and national legislation; and then traced the slavery and anti-slavery question down to the Rebellion. I became convinced that a history of the Colored people in America was required, because of the ample historically trustworthy material at hand; because the Colored people themselves had been the most vexatious problem in North America, from the time of its discovery down to the present day; because that in every attempt upon the life of the nation, whether by foes from without or within, the Colored people had always displayed a matchless patriotism and an incomparable heroism in the cause of Americans; and because such a history would give the world more correct ideas of the Colored people, and incite the latter to greater effort in the struggle of citizenship and manhood. The single reason that there was no history of the Negro race would have been a sufficient reason for writing one.

The labor incident upon the several public positions held by me precluded an earlier completion of this task; and, finding it absolutely impossible to write while discharging public duties or practising law, I retired from the public service several years ago, and since that time have devoted all my energies to this work. It is now nearly seven years since I began this wonderful task.

I have been possessed of a painful sense of the vastness of my work from first to last. I regret that for the sake of pressing the work into a single volume, favorable to a speedy sale, — at the sacrifice of the record of a most remarkable people, — I found my heart unwilling, and my best judgment protesting.

In the preparation of this work I have consulted over twelve thousand volumes, — about one thousand of which are referred to in the footnotes, — and thousands of pamphlets.

After wide and careful reading, extending through three years, I conceived the present plan of this history. I divided it into nine parts. Two thoughts led me to prepare the chapters under the head of PRELIMINARY CONSIDERATIONS. *First,* The defenders of slavery and the traducers of the Negro built their pro-slavery arguments upon biblical ethnology and the curse of Canaan. I am alive to the fact, that, while I am a believer in the Holy Bible, it is not the best authority on ethnology. As far as it goes, it is agreeable to my head and heart. Whatever science has added I have gladly appropriated. I make no claim, however, to be a specialist. While the curse of Canaan is no longer a question of debate, yet nevertheless the folly of the obsolete theory should be thoroughly understood by the young men of the Negro race who, though voting now, were not born when Sumter was fired upon. *Second,* A growing desire among the enlightened Negroes in America to learn all that is possible from research concerning the antiquity of the race, — Africa, its inhabitants, and the development of the Negro governments of Sierra Leone and Liberia, led me to furnish something to meet a felt need. If the Negro slave desired his native land before the Rebellion, will not the free, intelligent, and reflective American Negro turn to Africa with its problems of geography and missions, now that he can contribute something towards the improvement of the condition of humanity? Editors and writers everywhere throughout the world should spell the word Negro with a capital N ; and when referring to the race as Colored people employ a capital C. I trust this will be observed.

In PART II., SLAVERY IN THE COLONIES, I have striven to give a succinct account of the establishment and growth of slavery under the English Crown. It involved almost infinite labor to go to the records of "the original thirteen colonies." It is proper to observe that this part is one of great value and interest.

In PART III., THE NEGRO DURING THE REVOLUTION, I found much of an almost romantic character. Many traditions have been put down, and many obscure truths elucidated. Some persons may think it irreverent to tell the truth in the plain, homely manner that characterizes my narrative ; but, while I have nothing to regret in this particular, I can assure them that I have been actuated by none other spirit than that of candor. Where I have used documents it was with a desire to escape the charge of superficiality. If, however, I may be charged with seeking to escape the labor incident to thorough digestion, I answer, that, while men with the reputation of Bancroft and Hildreth could pass unchallenged when disregarding largely the use of documents and the citation of authorities, I would find myself challenged by a large number of critics. Moreover I have felt it would be almost cruel to mutilate some of the very rare old documents that shed such peerless light upon the subject in hand.

I have brought the first volume down to the close of the eighteenth century, detailing the great struggle through which the slavery problem passed. I have given as fair an idea of the debate on this question, in the convention that framed the Constitution, as possible. It was then and there that the hydra of slavery struck its fangs into the Constitution ; and, once inoculated with the poison of the monster, the government was only able to purify itself in the flames of a great civil war.

The second volume opens with the present century, and closes with the year 1880. Unable to destroy slavery by constitutional law, the best thought and effort of this period were directed against the extension of the evil into the territory beyond the Ohio, Mississippi, and Missouri rivers. But having placed three-fifths of the slave population under the Constitution, having pledged the Constitution to the protection of slave property, it required an almost superhuman effort to confine the evil to one section of the country. Like a loathsome disease it spread itself over the body politic until our nation became the eyesore of the age, and a byword among the nations of the world. The time came when our beloved country had to submit to heroic treatment, and the cancer of slavery was removed by the sword.

In giving an account of the *Anti-Slavery Agitation Movement,* I have found myself able to deal briefly with methods and results only. I have striven to honor all the multifarious measures adopted to save the Negro and the Nation. I have not attempted to write a history of the Anti-Slavery Movement. Many noble men and women have not even been mentioned. It should not be forgotten that this is a history of the Negro race; and as such I have not run into the topic discussed by the late Henry Wilson in his " Rise and Fall of the Slave Power."

In discussing the problem of the rendition of fugitive slaves by the Union army, I have given the facts with temperate and honest criticism. And, in recounting the sufferings Negro troops endured as prisoners of war in the hands of the Rebels, I have avoided any spirit of bitterness. A great deal of the material on the war I purchased from the MS. library of Mr. Thomas S. Townsend of New-York City. The questions of vital, prison, labor, educational, and financial statistics cannot fail to interest intelligent people of all races and parties. These statistics are full of comfort and assurance to the Negro as well as to his friends.

Every cabinet minister of the President wrote me full information upon all the questions I asked, and promptly too. The refusal of the general and adjutant-general of the army did not destroy my hope of getting some information concerning the Negro regiments in the regular army. I visited the Indian Territory, Kansas, Texas, and New Mexico, where I have seen the Ninth and Tenth Regiments of cavalry, and the Twenty-fourth Regiment of infantry. The Twenty-fifth Regiment of infantry is at Fort Randall, Dakota. These are among the most effective troops in the regular army. The annual desertions in white regiments of cavalry vary from ninety-eight to a hundred and eighteen; while in Negro regiments of cavalry the desertions only average from six to nine per annum. The Negro regiments are composed of young men, intelligent, faithful, brave. I heard but one complaint from the lips of a score of white officers I met, and that was that the Negroes sometimes struck their horses over the head.

Every distinction in law has disappeared, except in the regular army. Here Negroes are excluded from the artillery service and engineer's department. It is wrong, and Congress should place these brave black soldiers upon the same footing as the white troops.

I have to thank Drs. George H. Moore and S. Austin Allibone, of the Lenox Library, for the many kind favors shown me while pursuing my studies in New-York City. And I am under very great obligations to Dr. Moore for his admirable " History of Early Slavery in Massachusetts," without which I should have been put to great inconvenience. To Mr. John Austin Stevens, late editor of "The Magazine of American History," who, during several months residence in New-York City, placed his private library and office at my service, and did every thing in his power to aid my investigations, I return my sincerest thanks. To the Librarians of the New-York Historical, Astor, and New-York Society Libraries, I return thanks for favors shown, and privileges granted. I am especially grateful to the Hon. Ainsworth R. Spofford, Librarian of Congress, for the manner in which he facilitated my researches during my sojourn in Washington. I had the use of many newspapers of the last century, and of other material to be found only in the Congressional Library.

To Sir T. Risely Griffith, Colonial Secretary and Treasurer of Sierra Leone, I am indebted for valuable statistics concerning that colony.

To the Assistant Librarian of the State Library of Ohio, the accomplished and efficient Miss Mary C. Harbough, I owe more than to any other person. Through her unwavering and untiring kindness and friendship, I have been enabled to use five hundred and seventy-six volumes from that library, besides newspaper files and Congressional Records. To Gov. Charles Foster, Chairman of the Board of Library Commissioners, I offer my profoundest thanks for the intelligent, active, and practical interest he has taken in the completion of this work. And to Major Charles Townsend, Secretary of State, I offer thanks for favors shown me in securing documents. To the Rev. J. L. Grover and his competent assistant, Mr. Charles H. Bell, of the Public Library of Columbus, I am indebted for the use of many works. They cheerfully rendered whatever aid they could, and for their kindness I return many thanks.

I am obliged to the Rev. Benjamin W. Arnett, Financial Secretary of the A. M. E. Church of the United States, for the statistics of his denomination. And to all persons who have sent me newspapers and pamphlets

I desire to return thanks.   I am grateful to C. A. Fleetwood, an efficient clerk in the War Department, for statistics on the Freedmen's Bank.   And, above all and more than all, I return my profoundest thanks to my heavenly Father for the inspiration, health, and money by which I have been enabled to complete this great task.

I have mentioned such Colored men as I thought necessary.   To give a biographical sketch of all the worthy Colored men in the United States, would require more space than has been occupied in this work.

Not as the blind panegyrist of my race, nor as the partisan apologist, but from a love for "*the truth of history,*" I have striven to record the truth, the whole truth, and nothing but the truth.   I have not striven to revive sectional animosities or race prejudices.   I have avoided comment so far as it was consistent with a clear exposition of the truth.   My whole aim has been to write a thoroughly trustworthy history; and what I have written, if it have no other merit, is reliable.

I commit this work to the public, white and black, to the friends and foes of the Negro, in the hope that the obsolete antagonisms which grew out of the relation of master and slave may speedily sink as storms beneath the horizon; and that the day will hasten when there shall be no North, no South, no Black, no White, — but all be American citizens, with equal duties and equal rights.

GEORGE W. WILLIAMS.

New York, November, 1882.

CONTENTS.

xi

CHAPTER V.

THE ASHANTEE EMPIRE.

PAGE

CHAPTER VI.

THE NEGRO TYPE.

CHAPTER VII.

AFRICAN IDIOSYNCRASIES.

CHAPTER VIII.

LANGUAGES, LITERATURE, AND RELIGION.

CHAPTER IX.

SIERRA LEONE.

CHAPTER X.

THE REPUBLIC OF LIBERIA.

Part II.

SLAVERY IN THE COLONIES.

CHAPTER XIV.

THE COLONY OF MASSACHUSETTS.

1633-1775.

PAGE

CHAPTER XV.

THE COLONY OF MASSACHUSETTS, — CONTINUED.

1633-1775.

CHAPTER XVI.

THE COLONY OF MARYLAND.

1634-1775.

CHAPTER XVII.

THE COLONY OF DELAWARE.

1636-1775.

CHAPTER XVIII.

THE COLONY OF CONNECTICUT.

1646–1775.

CHAPTER XIX.

THE COLONY OF RHODE ISLAND.

1647–1775.

CHAPTER XX.

THE COLONY OF NEW JERSEY.

1664–1775.

Part III.

THE NEGRO DURING THE REVOLUTION.

CHAPTER XXVII.

NEGROES AS SOLDIERS.

1775–1783.

CHAPTER XXVIII.

LEGAL STATUS OF THE NEGRO DURING THE REVOLUTION.

1775–1783.

CHAPTER XXIX.

THE NEGRO INTELLECT. — BANNEKER THE ASTRONOMER. — FULLER THE MATHEMATICIAN. — DERHAM THE PHYSICIAN.

CHAPTER XXX.

SLAVERY DURING THE REVOLUTION.

1775–1783.

CHAPTER XXXI.

SLAVERY AS A POLITICAL AND LEGAL PROBLEM.

1775–1800.

HISTORY OF THE NEGRO RACE IN AMERICA.

Part I.

PRELIMINARY CONSIDERATIONS.

CHAPTER I.

THE UNITY OF MANKIND.

THE BIBLICAL ARGUMENT. — ONE RACE AND ONE LANGUAGE. — ONE BLOOD. — THE CURSE OF CANAAN.

DURING the last half-century, many writers on ethnology, anthropology, and slavery have strenuously striven to place the Negro outside of the human family; and the disciples of these teachers have endeavored to justify their views by the most dehumanizing treatment of the Negro. But, fortunately for the Negro and for humanity at large, we live now in an epoch when race malice and sectional hate are disappearing beneath the horizon of a brighter and better future. The Negro in America is free. He is now an acknowledged factor in the affairs of the continent; and no community, state, or government, in this period of the world's history, can afford to be indifferent to his moral, social, intellectual, or political well-being.

It is proposed, in the first place, to call the attention to the absurd charge that the Negro does not belong to the human family. Happily, there are few left upon the face of the earth who still maintain this belief.

In the first chapter of the Book of Genesis it is clearly stated that "God created man," "male and female created he them;"[1] that "the Lord God formed man of the dust of the ground, and

---

[1] Gen. i. 27.

breathed into his nostrils the breath of life; and man became a living soul;"[1] and that "the Lord God took the man, and put him into the Garden of Eden to dress it and to keep it."[2]   It is noticeable that the sacred historian, in every reference to Adam, speaks of him as "*man ;*" and that the divine injunction to them was, — Adam and Eve, — "Be fruitful, and multiply, and replenish the earth, and subdue it : and have dominion over the fish of the sea, and over the fowl of the air, and over every living thing that moveth upon the earth."[3]   As among the animals, so here in the higher order, there were two, — a pair, — "male and female," of the human species.   We may begin with man, and run down the scale, and we are sure to find two of a kind, "male and female." This was the divine order.   But they were to "be fruitful," were to "replenish the earth."   That they did "multiply," we have the trustworthy testimony of God ; and it was true that man and beast, fowl and fish, increased.   We read that after their expulsion from the Garden of Eden, Eve bore Adam a family, Cain and Abel ; and that they "peopled the earth."

After a number of years we find that wickedness increased in the earth ; so much so that the Lord was provoked to destroy the earth with a flood, with the exception of Noah, his wife, his three sons and their wives, — eight souls in all.[4]   Of the animals, two of each kind were saved.

But the most interesting portion of Bible history comes after the Flood.   We then have the history of the confusion of tongues, and the subsequent and consequent dispersion of mankind.   In the eleventh chapter and first verse of Genesis it is recorded : "*And the* WHOLE EARTH *was of* ONE LANGUAGE, *and of* ONE SPEECH.*"   "The whole earth" here means all the inhabitants of the earth, — all mankind.   The medium of communication was common.   Everybody used one language.   In the sixth verse occurs this remarkable language : "And the Lord said, Behold, the people is *one*, and they have all *one* language."   Attention is called to this verse, because we have here the testimony of the Lord that "the people is *one*," and that the language of the people is one.   This verse establishes two very important facts ; i.e., there was but one nationality, and hence but one language.   The fact that they had but one language furnishes reasonable proof that they were of one blood ; and the historian has covered the whole

---

[1] Gen. ii. 7.   [2] Gen. ii. 15.   [3] Gen. i. 28.   [4] Gen. vi. 5 *sq.*

question very carefully by recording the great truth that they were *one people*, and had but *one language*. The seventh, eighth, and ninth verses of the eleventh chapter are not irrelevant : " Go to, let us go down, and there confound their language, that they may not understand one another's speech. So the Lord scattered them abroad from thence upon the face of all the earth : and they left off to build the city. Therefore is the name of it called Babel ; because the Lord did there confound the language of all the earth : and from thence did the Lord scatter them abroad upon the face of all the earth."

It was the wickedness of the people that caused the Lord to disperse them, to confound their speech, and bring to nought their haughty work. Evidently this was the beginning of different families of men, — different nationalities, and hence different languages. In the ninth verse it reads, that "from thence did the Lord scatter them abroad upon the face of all the earth." There is no ambiguity about this language. He did not only "confound their language," but "scattered them from thence," from Babel, "upon the face of all the earth." Here, then, are two very important facts : their *language* was *confused*, and they *were* "*scattered*." They were not only "scattered," they were "scattered *abroad upon the face of all* the earth." That is, they were dispersed very widely, sent into the various and remote parts of the earth ; and their nationality received its being from the latitudes to which the divinely appointed wave of dispersion bore them ; and their subsequent racial character was to borrow its tone and color from climateric influences. Three great families, the Shemitic, Hamitic, and Japhetic, were suddenly built up. Many other families, or tribes, sprang from these ; but these were the three great heads of all subsequent races of men.

" That the three sons of Noah overspread and peopled the whole earth, is so expressly stated in Scripture, that, had we not to argue against those who unfortunately disbelieve such evidence, we might here stop : let us, however, inquire how far the truth of this declaration is substantiated by other considerations. Enough has been said to show that there is a curious, if not a remarkable, analogy between the predictions of Noah on the future descendants of his three sons, and the actual state of those races which are generally supposed to have sprung from them. It may here be again remarked, that, to render the subject more clear, we have adopted the quinary arrangement of Professor Blumenbach : yet that Cuvier and other learned physiologists are of opinion that the primary varieties of the human form are more properly but three ; viz., the Caucasian, Mongolian, and Ethiopian. This number corresponds with that of Noah's sons. Assigning, therefore, the Mongolian race to Japheth, and the Ethiopian to Ham, the Caucasian, the noblest race, will belong to Shem, the third son of Noah, himself descended from Seth, the third son of Adam. That the primary distinctions of the human varieties are but *three*, has been further maintained by the erudite Prichard; who, while he rejects the nomenclature both of Blumenbach and Cuvier, as implying absolute divisions, arranges the leading varieties of the human skull under three sections, differing from those of Cuvier only by name. That the three sons of Noah who were to 'replenish the earth,' and on whose progeny very opposite destinies were pronounced, should give birth to different races, is what might reasonably be conjectured; but that the observation of those who do, and of those who do not, believe the Mosaic history, should tend to confirm truth, by pointing out in what these three races do actually differ, both physically and morally, is, to say the least, a singular coincidence. It amounts, in short, to a presumptive evidence, that a mysterious and very beautiful analogy pervades throughout, and teaches us to look beyond natural causes in attempting to account for effects apparently interwoven in the plans of Omnipotence."[1]

In the seventeenth chapter of the Acts of the Apostles, twenty-sixth verse, we find the following language: "And hath made of one blood all nations of men for to dwell on all the face of the earth, and hath determined the times before appointed, and the bounds of their habitation."[2] The Apostle Paul was a missionary. He was, at this time, on a mission to the far-famed city of Athens, — "the eye of Greece, and the fountain of learning and philosophy." He told the "men of Athens," that, as he travelled through their beautiful city, he had not been unmindful of its attractions; that he had not been indifferent to the claims of its citizens to scholarship and culture, and that among other things he noticed an altar erected to *an unknown God.* He went on to remark, that, great as their city and nation were, God, whose offspring they were, had created other nations, who lived beyond their verdant hills and swelling rivers. And, moreover, that God had created "all nations of men for to dwell on all the face of the earth" out "of one blood." He called their attention to the fact that God had fenced all the nations in by geographical boundaries, — had fixed the limits of their habitation.

We find two leading thoughts in the twenty-sixth verse; viz.,

---

[1] Encycl. of Geo., p. 255.

[2] If the Apostle Paul had asserted that all men resembled each other in the color of their skin and the texture of their hair, or even in their physiological make-up, he would have been at war with observation and critical investigation. But, having announced a wonderful truth in reference to the unity of the human race as based upon one blood, science comes to his support, and through the microscope reveals the corpuscles of the blood, and shows that the globule is the same in all human blood.

that this passage establishes clearly and unmistakably the unity of mankind, in that God created them of one blood; second, he hath determined "the bounds of their habitation," — hath located them geographically. The language quoted is very explicit. "He hath determined the bounds of their habitation," that is, " all the nations of men.[1] We have, then, the fact, that there are different "nations of men," and that they are all "of one blood," and, therefore, have a common parent. This declaration was made by the Apostle Paul, an inspired writer, a teacher of great erudition, and a scholar in both the Hebrew and the Greek languages.

It should not be forgotten either, that in Paul's masterly discussion of the doctrine of sin, — the fall of man, — he always refers to Adam as the "one man" by whom sin came into the world.[2] His Epistle to the Romans abounds in passages which prove very plainly the unity of mankind. The Acts of the Apostles, as well as the Gospels, prove the unity we seek to establish.

But there are a few who would admit the unity of mankind, and still insist that the Negro does not belong to the human family. It is so preposterous, that one has a keen sense of humiliation in the assured consciousness that he goes rather low to meet the enemies of God's poor; but it can certainly do no harm to meet them with the everlasting truth.

In the Gospel of Luke we read this remarkable historical statement: "And as they led him away, they laid hold upon one Simon, a Cyrenian, coming out of the country, and on him they laid the cross, that he might bear it after Jesus."[3] By referring to the map, the reader will observe that Cyrene is in Libya, on the north coast of Africa. All the commentators we have been able to consult, on the passage quoted below, agree that this man Simon was a Negro, — a black man. John Melville produced a very remarkable sermon from this passage.[4] And many of the most celebrated pictures of "The Crucifixion," in Europe, represent this Cyrenian as black, and give him a very prominent place in the most tragic scene ever witnessed on this earth. In the Acts

---

[1] Deut. xxxii. 8, 9: "When the Most High divided to the nations their inheritance, when he separated the sons of Adam, he set the bounds of the people according to the number of the children of Israel. For the Lord's portion is his people; Jacob is the lot of his inheritance."

[2] Rom. v. 12, 14-21.

[3] Luke xxiii. 26; Acts vi. 9, also second chapter, tenth verse. Matthew records the same fact in the twenty-seventh chapter, thirty-second verse: "And as they came out, they found a man of Cyrene, Simon by name: him they compelled to bear his cross."

[4] See Melville's Sermons.

of the Apostles we have a very full and interesting account of the conversion and immersion of the Ethiopian eunuch, "a man of Ethiopia, an eunuch of great authority under Candace, Queen of the Ethiopians, who had the charge of all her treasure, and had come to Jerusalem for to worship."[1] Here, again, we find that all the commentators agree as to the nationality of the eunuch : he was a Negro; and, by implication, the passage quoted leads us to the belief that the Ethiopians were a numerous and wealthy people. Candace was the queen that made war against Augustus Cæsar twenty years before Christ, and, though not victorious, secured an honorable peace.[2] She reigned in Upper Egypt, — up the Nile, — and lived at Meroe, that ancient city, the very cradle of Egyptian civilization.[3]

"In the time of our Saviour (and indeed from that time forward), by Ethiopia was meant, in a general sense, the countries south of Egypt, then but imperfectly known ; of one of which that Candace was queen whose eunuch was baptized by Philip. Mr. Bruce, on his return from Abyssinia, found in latitude 16° 38' a place called Chendi, where the reigning sovereign was then a queen ; and where a tradition existed that a woman, by name Hendaque (which comes as near as possible to the Greek name Χανδακη), once governed all that country. Near this place are extensive ruins, consisting of broken pedestals and obelisks, which Bruce conjectures to be those of Meroe, the capital of the African Ethiopia, which is described by Herodotus as a great city in his time, namely, four hundred years before Christ; and where, separated from the rest of the world by almost impassable deserts, and enriched by the commercial expeditions of their travelling brethren, the Cushites continued to cultivate, so late as the first century of the Christian era, some portions of those arts and sciences to which the settlers in the cities had always more or less devoted themselves."[4]

But a few writers have asserted, and striven to prove, that the Egyptians and Ethiopians are quite a different people from the Negro. Jeremiah seems to have understood that these people about whom we have been writing were Negroes, — we mean black. "Can the Ethiopian," asks the prophet, "change his skin, or the leopard his spots?" The prophet was as thoroughly aware that the Ethiopian was black, as that the leopard had spots; and Luther's German has for the word "Ethiopia," "Negro-land," —

---

[1] Acts viii. 27.
[2] Pliny says the Ethiopian government subsisted for several generations in the hands of queens whose name was *Candace*.
[3] See Liddell and Scott's Greek Lexicon.
[4] Jones's Biblical Cyclopædia, p. 311.

the country of the blacks.[1] The word "Ethiop" in the Greek literally means "sunburn."

That these Ethiopians were black, we have, in addition to the valuable testimony of Jeremiah, the scholarly evidence of Herodotus, Homer, Josephus, Eusebius, Strabo, and others.

It will be necessary for us to use the term "Cush" farther along in this discussion : so we call attention at this time to the fact, that the Cushites, so frequently referred to in the Scriptures, are the same as the Ethiopians.

Driven from unscriptural and untenable ground on the unity of the races of mankind, the enemies of the Negro, falling back in confusion, intrench themselves in the curse of Canaan. "And Noah awoke from his wine, and knew what his younger son had done unto him. And he said, Cursed be Canaan ; a servant of servants shall he be unto his brethren." [2] This passage was the leading theme of the defenders of slavery in the pulpit for many years. Bishop Hopkins says, —

"The heartless irreverence which Ham, the father of Canaan, displayed toward his eminent parent, whose piety had just saved him from the Deluge, presented the immediate *occasion* for this remarkable prophecy; but the actual *fulfilment* was reserved for his posterity after they had lost the knowledge of God, and become utterly polluted by the abominations of heathen idolatry. The Almighty, foreseeing this total degradation of the race, ordained them to servitude or slavery under the descendants of Shem and Japheth, doubtless because *he judged it to be their fittest condition.* And all history proves how accurately the prediction has been accomplished, even to the present day." [3]

Now, the first thing to be done by those who adopt this view is, to prove, beyond a reasonable doubt, that Noah was inspired to pronounce this prophecy. Noah *had* been, as a rule, a righteous man. For more than a hundred years he had lifted up his voice against the growing wickedness of the world. His fidelity to the cause of God was unquestioned ; and for his faith and correct living, he and his entire household were saved from the Deluge. But after his miraculous deliverance from the destruction that overcame the old world, his entire character is changed. There is not a single passage to show us that he continued his avocation as a preacher. He became a husbandman ; he kept a vineyard ; and, more than all, he drank of the wine and got drunk !

---

[1] The term Ethiope was anciently given to all those whose color was darkened by the sun. — *Smyth's Unity of the Human Races*, chap. i. p. 34.

[2] Gen. ix. 24, 25. See also the twenty-sixth and twenty-seventh verses.

[3] Bible Views of Slavery, p. 7.

Awaking from a state of inebriation, he knew that Ham had beheld his nakedness and "told his two brethren." But "Shem and Japheth took a garment, and laid it upon both their shoulders, and went backward, and covered the nakedness of their father ; and their faces were backward, and they saw not their father's nakedness." [1]   It is quite natural to suppose, that, humiliated and chagrined at his sinful conduct, and angered at the behavior of his son and grandson, Ham and Canaan, Noah expressed his disapprobation of Canaan.   It was *his* desire, on the impulse of the moment, that Canaan should suffer a humiliation somewhat commensurate with his offence ; and, on the other hand, it was appropriate that he should commend the conduct of his other sons, who sought to hide their father's shame.   And all this was done without any inspiration.   He simply expressed himself as a fallible man.

Bishop Hopkins, however, is pleased to call this a "prophecy." In order to prophesy, in the scriptural meaning of the word, a man must have the divine unction, and must be moved by the Holy Ghost ; and, in addition to this, it should be said, that a true prophecy always comes to pass, — is sure of fulfilment.   Noah was not inspired when he pronounced his curse against Canaan, for the sufficient reason that it was not fulfilled.   He was not speaking in the spirit of prophecy when he blessed Shem and Japheth, for the good reason that their descendants have often been in bondage.   Now, if these words of Noah were prophetic, were inspired of God, we would naturally expect to find *all of Canaan's descendants in bondage*, and all of Shem's out of bondage, — free!   If this prophecy — granting this point to the learned bishop for argument's sake — has not been fulfilled, then we conclude one of two things ; namely, these are not the words of God, or they have not been fulfilled.   But they were not the words of prophecy, and consequently never had any divine authority.   It was Canaan upon whom Noah pronounced the curse : and Canaan was the son of Ham ; and Ham, it is said, is the progenitor of the Negro race.   The Canaanites were not bondmen, but freemen, — powerful tribes when the Hebrews invaded their country ; and from the Canaanites descended the bold and intelligent Carthaginians, as is admitted by the majority of writers on this subject.   From Ham proceeded the Egyptians, Libyans, the Phu-

---

[1]   Gen. ix. 23.